Are You Ready, Freddie? Err...Ruff!

Written by Dorothy Scott, EdD

Illustrated by Bob Scott

Copyright © 2019 by Dorothy Scott, EdD

Illustration Copyright © 2019 by Bob Scott

All rights reserved.
No part of this publication may be reproduced or transmitted in any form
or by any means, electronical, mechanical, photocopying, recording or
otherwise, without the express written permission of the author.

Printed on Demand by Amazon
E book available on Kindle For Kids

The artwork was created with Windsor Newton Sable brush and India Ink on Bristol
Text is set in Georgia Text

Book layout by Vicki Scott

For Freddie,
an old dog with lots of new tricks.

Freddie never wants to get up in the morning.
"Time to get up. You can't sleep all day."

When Freddie gets up,
he always needs to go potty.
"Let's go for a walk."

Freddie meets and plays with his friends at the park.

"Are you ready, Freddie?"

ERR... **RUFF!**

After breakfast Freddie
always looks for more food.
"How about a treat?"

Going for a walk and eating all that food
makes Freddie very tired.
"Time for a nap."

"Are you ready, Freddie?"

Errr... Ruff!

Freddie likes to talk and he talks a lot,
especially when he's hungry!

"Are you ready, Freddie?"

ERR...RUFF! ERR...RUFF!

ERR...RUFF! ERR...RUFF!

ERR...RUFF! ERR...RUFF!

In the evening Freddie likes to go for a ride in the car.
"Let's go get some ice cream."

"Are you ready, Freddie?"

ERR... RUFF!

After eating ice cream Freddie's tummy is full,
and he always falls asleep.
"Wake up, Freddie.
Time to get out of the car."

"Are you ready, Freddie?"

Often times Freddie gets dirty.
"Time for a bath."

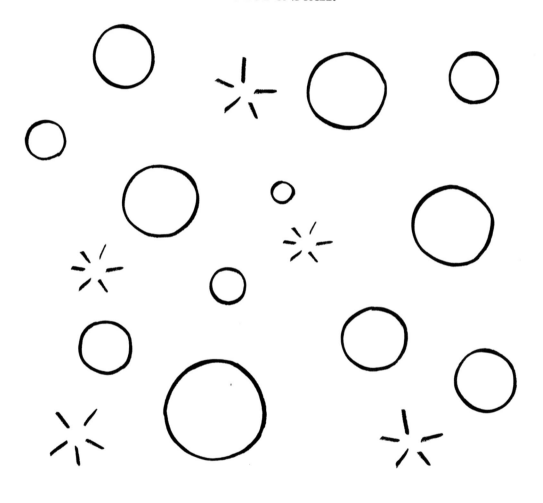

After Freddie's bath, he always likes to
shake, shake, shake
the water off!

Sleeping is Freddie's favorite thing to do,
especially when it is right between Mommy and Daddy
where he is warm and cozy.

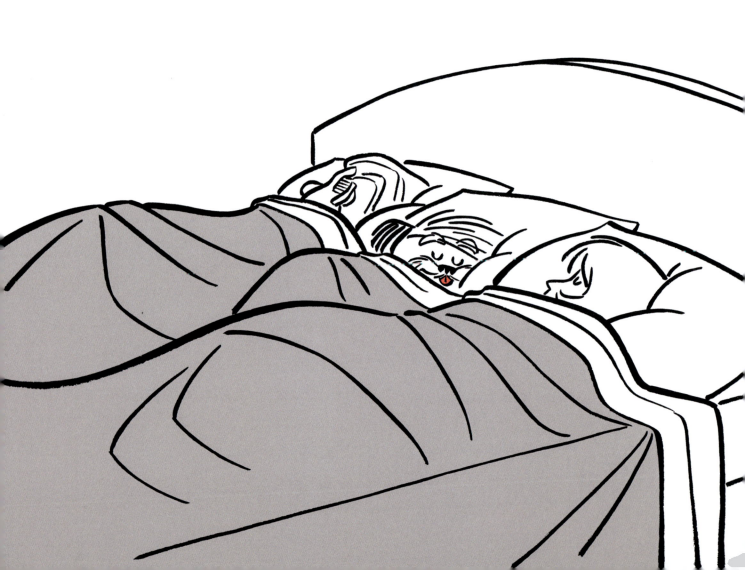

"Are you ready, Freddie?"

ERR...RUFF!
ERR...RUFF...RUFF!

ZZZZZZzzzz

Are You Ready, Freddie Err...Ruff!
stars Freddie, Dorothy's own dog.
She fell in love with Freddie when she found
him in the Animal Shelter. Skinny, lonely and very
old, Freddie needed a lot of care, so Dorothy swept
him into her arms and gave him his forever home.
She hopes this picture book will inspire others
to adopt older shelter animals.

Sometimes a little love changes everything!

Thank you for reading my book.

I hope you have enjoyed reading
Are You Ready, Freddie? Errr...Ruff!
as much as I enjoyed writing it!

If you have a moment, please post a review on amazon.com,
talk to your family and friends about this book,
or suggest it to your local schools.

I am ready for everyone to see this book!

Errr...Ruff!

Made in the USA
Columbia, SC
07 June 2019